Then and Now

by Sasha Griffin

illustrated by Ginna Magee

PEARSON

Scott
Foresman

Editorial Offices: Glenview, Illinois • Parsippany, New Jersey • New York, New York
Sales Offices: Needham, Massachusetts • Duluth, Georgia • Glenview, Illinois
Coppell, Texas • Ontario, California • Mesa, Arizona

Here I am when I was a baby.

Everything about me was so small!

Then I could not stand up.

Now I can run and jump.

Then Mom and Dad fed me.

Now I am the one who feeds me.

Then I did a lot of crying.

Now I always ask for the things I want.

Then I could not stay awake for long.

Now I can play all day.

7

Then I did nothing by myself.

I like that I have become a big kid now!